INVITED JOB INTERVIEW?

NOW WHAT?

How to Succeed at Your Next Interview

Claire B Jenkins

&

Dr Anita Pickerden

Illustrations by Anna Geyer

Publishing in the United Kingdom by:
Ingram Spark

Illustrations by Anna Geyer

Book design & layout by Velin@Perseus-Design.com

ISBN Number: 978-1-9997654-0-8 (Paperback)

CONTENTS

This book is designed to help you be successful at your next interview.

It aims to offer practical advice, tips and simple exercises to improve your interview preparation techniques.

Our goal is to show how small changes can have a significant impact on how you present both yourself and what you have to offer your potential new employer.

We'll try to keep it as simple as possible, e.g. we'll ask you to use or think of *just 3 things* quite a lot during this book because it's easy to remember and can save a lot of head scratching trying to think of long lists of things to work on. Three is an easier starting point.

Trying out a more focused approach, and using the suggestions here, will be a key part of building good habits for when your next interview invite arrives.

1. PREPARATION

- what to think about and how to prepare

Congratulations! You've been offered an interview.

This is great news because someone, at least one person, thinks you can do the job.

Now it's time to improve your approach to interviews and increase your chances of securing that job offer.

Here's what we'll cover:-

We'll start by helping you to think and behave more confidently about your interview, and then move on to how to do your research so that you are really well prepared. We mean "research" not only on the company and the sector, but also on how you are going to anticipate the questions and plan your answers.

We all know that sometimes things don't go to plan, so we'll also discuss how to deal with disappointment - just in case you don't get the job.

Can I do this job?

You have an invite to interview so now the key question is - do <u>you</u> believe you can do the job?

Are you a great "fit" to the role or, if you get the job, will you feel like an "imposter"?

It's worth remembering that many of us have felt varying degrees of this throughout our lives.

Some very famous names have confessed to feeling this way; Emma Watson, Michelle Pfeiffer, Denzel Washington and even the late Maya Angelou. The American author and poet once said 'I have written eleven books, but each time I think, "Uh oh...they're going to find me out."'

There's an excellent technique to help you to get over this; it's called "positive self-talk" and we'll be explaining that in the next section.

Getting your head right

Confidence

Having the right "Mindset" is crucially important. Now let's consider how to get your head around feeling ready to "perform" at your best at your next interview.

Start by thinking back to how you've done before at previous interviews or in similar circumstances. Try to recall what it was like when you had to tell someone you've only just met something significant about yourself.

This doesn't necessarily mean a job interview. It could be when you had to give a presentation or attend a formal meeting at school, college or even an informal chat to secure a voluntary role or a part time job.

You may have been out of work for a while, or perhaps you haven't had an interview for quite a long time. Cast your mind back to the last time you felt you were similarly in the spotlight to "perform".

EXERCISE

Make a list of your last 3 interviews or "interview-like" experiences:

1

2

3

If you've used situations that are "interview-like" use a few key words here to explain why they were similar:

....

....

....

What do these experiences tell you about how your next interview might go?

....

....

....

What did you do really well?

. . . .

. . . .

. . . .

Where could you have done better? (Be as honest as you can with yourself if you're really going to use the experience to your advantage.)

. . . .

. . . .

. . . .

What questions did they ask you? It's worth jotting these down and thinking about what an ideal answer might be for each of them.

. . . .

. . . .

. . . .

Forget what you said in reply at the time and look at them now with a "fresh pair of eyes". How could you have responded differently, now that you aren't under pressure?

. . . .

. . . .

. . . .

Using "Positive Self-talk"

This is a really useful technique to help you increase your confidence.

We all have a version of a "voice" in our head that can reinforce how we feel about ourselves. Sometimes we even say these things out loud so we and others hear them too.

And it can be positive or negative: you can use self-talk to build up or to undermine your self-confidence. We need to actively avoid saying things like *"I'm stupid"*, *"I'll never get that job"*, *"I'm bound to mess this up"*, *"I'm scared of presentations"*, or *"I know my mind will go blank as soon as they ask the first question"*

So let's think about how to turn these into positive sentences like *"I can do this!"*, *"next time I'll ensure I..."*, *"I know I've nailed the preparation for this one"*, etc.

Listen to what you say to other people about yourself. Ask yourself what sort of things you say about yourself to your friends and family. Are those things positive and uplifting, or negative and downbeat?

When we're coaching people we often hear our clients saying things like, *"Yes, that's a good idea but my problem is ...."* Or *"I've never been any good at ..."* Well you've just proved to us that you're very good at negative self-talk – because you now believe this stuff! Now let's turn that around.

So, let's see if we can change your mind by altering what you say to yourself. You might want to acknowledge your fear of presentations, for example, by saying *"I <u>used to</u> avoid public speaking and now I've done more* *of it my presentation skills are much better"*. Next time, try saying to yourself "I'm good at this", "my presentation skills are much better than they used to be".

Put that negative voice behind you. Even using the past tense "I used to..." or "previously I've...". You'll be amazed how empowering this can sound to you and to those listening to you.

There are a couple of basic rules for positive self-talk:-

- Try to keep your comments in the present tense, e.g. *"I am good at this" "I can deliver a very effective presentation"*

- Word things in the positive: say *"I'm feeling confident"* because if you say *"don't be scared"* your brain may only hear "be scared"

You'll find some more information on self-talk in the Resources section at the end of the book.

Be Brave

What if I don't meet every single aspect of the job requirements?

Sometimes companies use a longer list than really necessary in the job advert to make the amount of applications they have to sift from more manageable. Be persistent. After all we know that possessing a certain qualification isn't always a reflection of your ability to do the job.

So when you're preparing for your interview, don't worry if you don't tick every box. Be truthful (always!) and then emphasise all the other things you've done that are relevant. And remember that your skills are often "transferrable" to lots of other situations so make it as easy as possible for the person shortlisting to understand how your experience matches what they're looking for.

For example, if you've spent the last few years at home parenting small children, you've got plenty of expertise in persuasion, negotiation, budgeting, crisis management, organisation and planning, decision making...... the list is endless!

Or if you've spent many years in retail and now want to move into office work, then your transferrable skills will probably include great communication, good customer service, punctuality and reliability.

This way, when you're asked questions about your experience, you can use examples from your previous work, and explain how they fit the current job role.

We recently coached a client who had been made redundant 3 times in different industries and was very worried that this would damage his chances of succeeding at interview. We were able to help him describe this as a "selling point" because he could bring lots of experience from different sectors, all of which would help his future employer. He felt much more confident knowing that he had a good "story" to tell, and contacted us to say he'd got the job. He was also able to show that his experiences demonstrated his resilience and adaptability (which is what a lot of employers want).

Apply the same thinking to your decisions about whether or not to even submit an application in the first place.

Sometimes recruiters may say they only want to select people who completely fulfil a job spec, while individual companies are often more open-minded. They'll want to see what talent is available and might select you for interview because of your more diverse experience. However, a lot will depend on how you describe what you can bring in terms of skills, experience and knowledge on your CV / Résumé or application.

What if the job you're applying for is much better paid than your current job? Recruiters will sometimes ask you about your current salary, thinking that it somehow describes what you're "worth". You don't always have to disclose your current pay, and what you were paid 5 or 10 years ago is hardly relevant today.

Avoid being put off by a much higher salary – if you think you can do the job then just put in an application and walk into the interview believing you can do it. The same applies if you're aiming for a lower paid job because you want a little less responsibility. Just be positive and honest about what you have to offer. The message that comes across loud and clear is *"if you're not sure, then apply anyway"*.

Body language

The adage goes "you only get one chance to make a first impression" so let's think about body language and how you present yourself to your audience at first glance.

Lots has been written about the power of a good "first impression". Even when interviewers are well-trained they may still give better scores to the people who make a strong impact right from the start. So the 'rapport-building stage' of the interview; walking in, smiling and shaking hands is very important for your success.

For the purposes of this book let's assume that your interviewers are more skilled and will genuinely listen to what you have to tell them. Now let's make sure you make a good first impression.

Practise how you will enter the interview room. As you put your hand onto the door handle, put a big smile on your face. As you walk in, make eye contact and smile at each member of the interview panel. Shake hands and sit down, ready for business. You may be nervous so aim to think of excitement rather than anxiety.

Shaking hands: - When being interviewed in a culture where shaking hands is the business "punctuation" of a meeting or interview, have a "good handshake" and use it at the beginning and at the end to make a good first and last impression on your audience. By "good handshake" we mean with a firm and dry grip. (If you have a tendency to sweaty palms, then carry a tissue in your pocket to use just as you enter the room.)

Ask friends who you think are business-like in their approach for some constructive feedback on what your handshake is like. This may sound a little strange although you'll thank us for suggesting it if it helps you create a great first impression.

If you're asked to deliver a presentation during your interview then make sure you are very well-prepared. For instance, adopt a confident manner while you present. If it's possible to do so then stand up - as it will help you to feel more confident. (If you have to remain seated then sit up straight!)

Sometimes the presentation topic isn't given until the day of the interview, so it's worthwhile thinking about what "story" you would like to get across. Think about how you'll demonstrate your understanding of the business and the sector (more about this later).

You may have heard of Amy Cuddy. She's an academic who has specialized in how our body language can affect our mood. Most of us used to think that it was the other way around – that our mood would affect our body language. Take a look at her TED Talk and you'll get lots of tips to help you walk into the interview room with great confidence (even if that's not how you're feeling). https://www.ted.com/talks/amy_cuddy_your_body_language_shapes_who_you_are

EXERCISE:

Try a "power pose" the next time you want to be calm and relaxed before you have an important meeting or presentation to make.

How useful did you find it?

. . . .

. . . .

. . . .

3 ways it might help me perform next time?

1.

2.

3.

What to wear

Find out what the accepted corporate "uniform" and generally accepted dress code / style is beforehand if you can.

If you're not sure, then wear something slightly more formal than you might have initially thought. Better to feel slightly "over-dressed" than the alternative. Being smartly dressed is also a mark of respect for your interviewers. And at the very least, make sure that your clothes are smart and neatly pressed, and your shoes are clean.

Wear things that you know you look good in and that will make you feel great. Smart clothing can really boost your confidence. Ensure you look professional and comfortable; if your shoes are painful it might show in your face!

Also important is how you smell: obviously be clean, but go easy on the perfume or after-shave. You don't want to knock your interviewer out as you walk into the room! Try asking for some honest feedback from people who know you well.

Consider how much you will "look like" your audience. We all connect with people similar to ourselves. This means employers have a tendency to choose people who are similar to them. Balance this carefully with your need to feel confident and authentic.

At the beginning of your career you probably don't want to hear this - and yet it really is true. The more you can look and sound like your interviewers the easier it will be for them to picture you doing the job. It's annoying ...and it's true.

Some employers are more enlightened and select and train their interviewers to overcome this tendency to employ "more of the same". Others are encouraged to do this to comply with legislation e.g. the Equality Act 2010 in the UK. However many still allow what's called "unconscious bias" to play too large a role in whom they appoint. This limits their ability to diversify their workforce and to celebrate the benefits that different perspectives and experiences can bring… but it still happens when "new" is perceived as potentially "risky" or "threatening".

However, this advice about looking similar to your audience has one big caveat. You also need to have something with you that's visually memorable.

When the panel have had a long day interviewing lots of people it'll help if they can distinguish one candidate from another when they're discussing them with their fellow interviewers:

"Was that the candidate with the fancy pen / distinctive tie / smart handbag / red scarf / memorable piece of jewellery, etc.?"

EXERCISE:

Plan what you'll wear to your next interview, get those clothes out of the wardrobe and try them on.

- Do they fit? Do they make me feel confident?

- Do they need washing or dry cleaning?

- Are the shoes polished?

- If not, then take action now, rather than rushing to do this on the morning of the interview.

- Decide what you're going to take with you: e.g a smart folder or note book with a prioritised list of key words to remind you of your best "skill stories" / interview answer examples and the questions you want to ask your interviewer, portfolio material with examples of your work, qualifications and references / recommendations?

- What will you have with you that will be visually different from other candidates?

2. DO YOUR RESEARCH

Whatever you do, turn up to the interview having done your "homework". If not you'll be wasting the interviewers' time as well as your own. The more research you do beforehand, the better prepared you'll feel, and you'll also make a much better impression on the interview panel.

For example, you might want to check on your LinkedIn contacts to see if you have any connections that work for your target organisation. They may even be able to give you some insight into the company before you're interviewed.

Preparing for the interview

If any of these details are unclear in the invitation to interview, then ask questions beforehand and well in advance of the day. Most recruiters and HR people are quite happy to answer any queries you may have. After all - it's in their interests to have well-prepared candidates.

Take as much potential "surprise" out of the day as you can. This will help you feel calm and prepared.

Here are some starting points for a checklist to help you.

a. When and where is it? If there's travel involved then check your route to the venue and make sure you arrive at least 15 minutes before the interview.

b. If you can, find out a bit about the room you'll be in - although don't worry if you can't find this out

c. How many people are interviewing you? Will it be one to one or with a panel?

d. Who's interviewing you? If you have their names then look them up on e.g. LinkedIn so that you recognise them and call them by their name.

e. What can you find out about them? (This is to reassure yourself and not for "name dropping" / "subject, college or workplace dropping")

f. What kind of interview will it be - knowledge / skills / experience / competency / behavioural? (see the Resources section for typical questions)

g. Or "Strengths" based? (Less likely) (see the Resources section for more detail of what they are, why they were developed, who uses them, what to expect, etc.)

h. How long should you expect it to last?

i. Is there anything you can prepare beforehand? If you're giving a presentation then check to see what IT facilities will be available. (Will they have a laptop and projector for you to use? Is it Windows or Apple software, etc? If in any doubt – take your own IT.)

j. If it's an internet / telephone based interview, then check that your technology works.

k. If you're going to be telephone interviewed at home please ensure there are no distractions or interruptions and that the mobile phone signal / Wi-Fi is good. Use whatever method will give the best sound quality. This might be FaceTime audio, a landline or another method so do a trial run to check for clarity.

l. Is it a "first interview" with the potential to get you a second one if you're successful initially?

m. Will there be any tests?

n. They might want you to do a numeracy, literacy, personality, I.T, "in tray" test, to give a presentation / introduce yourself to a group, to take part in a group discussion or team task, or even a role play exercise. Take some time to prepare for these and practise some beforehand. There are online ones to try or reference books you can use for all of these.

o. Is it an "Assessment Centre"? This tends to be a half or full day of tests, and is often used if there are a large number of applicants such as for an intern / graduate trainee / air steward / police role or if it's a well-known company that always attracts lots of candidates.

These tests should all be relevant to the vacancy and measuring the skills you'll need for the post - even if this may not be apparent at first.

p. Is it a more complicated interview? e.g. Multiple Mini Interviews (MMIs) This is more like a carousel format where you visit several "stations / desks" each one testing a different skill or competence. These are often used for medical or veterinary type roles and they're called things like "7 times 9" - indicating that you'll have seven tests each of 9 minutes in length.

Your interview may include some or all of the tests listed above. Remember also that they may well be observing you between the tests or even over meal or drinks breaks to see how you interact with others. So be on your 'best behaviour' at all times and imagine the interview starts as you arrive at the venue. Be polite to everyone you meet in the company. This is because you may not know the significance of someone you chat to in a corridor or over a coffee. Sometimes the decision makers will ask the receptionist and other staff what they thought of you.

EXERCISE:

Consider each of the questions a) to p) above, jotting down your answers and see whether there are some areas where you need to do some further research.

If so, start that planning now.

3 Things I need to know more about are:

1.

2.

3.

The sector

What do you know about the sector or sectors you want to get a job in?

Remember your role may encompass more than one e.g. Retail and I.T - you need to do your homework about both.

➤ What are the hot topics?

➤ What are the current trends / future issues facing the sector?

➤ Has there been anything in the news about them recently?

If you want to be even more thorough, do a SWOT or PESTLE analysis about the sector(s) and how your target organisation fits into them.

A **SWOT analysis** enables you to consider the Strengths, Weaknesses, Opportunities and Threats that are currently facing that employment sector. This will help you decide whether you want to work in it, and will also give you more to talk about at interview.

For example, in the Banking sector you could say that the size and longevity of the banks is a Strength, however the impact of any potential future political changes could be a Threat. Have a look at www.mindtools.com for an explanation and advice about how to use this methodology. You might want to finish your SWOT analysis with Opportunities to give you a positive conclusion.

A **PESTLE analysis** helps you to look at the various external influences and their impact on a business or a sector, so that you can research what challenges they may face in the short / medium / long term.

- **Political** factors are all about how, and to what degree, a government intervenes in the economy. This can include the impacts of government policy; national / regional / local, political stability or instability in overseas markets, foreign trade policy, tax policy, labour laws, environmental law, trade restrictions.

- **Economic** factors may alter how an organisation does business and also how profitable they are. Factors include economic growth, interest rates, exchange rates, inflation, as well as the levels of disposable income of consumers and businesses.

- **Social** factors include population growth, age distribution, health consciousness, career attitudes and demographic changes, etc.

- **Technological** factors include all of the changes related to scientific, medical, or ITC / software advances etc. They cover how a product or service is made, distributed and used.

- **Legal** factors can include health and safety, equal opportunities, advertising standards, consumer rights and laws, product labelling and product safety. If an organisation trades globally this is more complex because each country may have its own set of rules and regulations.

- **Environmental** factors have become important due to the increasing scarcity of raw materials, pollution targets, global warming as well as issues related to doing business in an ethical and sustainable way. This is often included in a company's "Corporate Social Responsibility" policies. (Or even their "Buzzword Bingo" - see the next section)

EXERCISE:

Conduct a PESTLE analysis on your target employer / organisation to see what the external influences are. This will help you to gather information about them.

For example, they may be having a 'problem' for which you can present yourself as the 'solution' at interview.

The organisation

What do they say about themselves and how they like to work? Check out their website and social media to understand their corporate values and behaviours. They're likely to have a section about what they've recently achieved, or an award, or to say that they are the biggest … or the best ….in a specific field.

Is there a published strategic plan for the organisation? What are their Priorities? How are they performing? Are they expanding into new markets?

What is their "problem" that filling this vacancy will solve? Do they have too much work, someone just leaving, a new project? Can you describe yourself in a way that solves this challenge?

Are you clear on the location of the job / geographic coverage of the role? And if the job is located in a different area, then can you travel there easily?

If they're a reasonably large organisation then you might find a lot of helpful information on www.glassdoor.co.uk, where people can post their own experiences (good and bad) of the company and of their interview processes.

"Buzzword Bingo": every organisation has its own buzzwords and jargon, so it's useful to familiarise yourself with some of this.

EXERCISE:

Make a list of all the information you've been able to find about your target organisation.

E.g What 'buzzwords" or jargon phrases are repeated in their corporate information? Where or who could help you understand what they really mean?

Where are they expanding? What are their priorities at present / in the near future?

The job

Read everything you have about the job!

It may sound obvious, however many people forget to use what they've been given already - it's likely to contain all the "clues" you'll need to get yourself started.

Advertisement - What did the job advert say they were looking for?

If there is one, then start your research with the **person specification**.

It's likely to be a bullet-point list of key words against which you've been shortlisted. The good news, as we mentioned in Chapter 1, is that the recruiters already think these match what you can offer them, because they've invited you to the interview.

Pay particular attention to whether they list an element as "desirable" as opposed to "essential". This is where the "bonus points" can be scored and may mean you have an advantage over other candidates.

Does it explain at what stage(s) in the process they expect you to demonstrate the skills and knowledge they list? For example, some employers will put letters next to the skills needed so they can be sure that you fit the job: often these letters are used as abbreviations "A" for application, "I" for interview, "R" for references, "T" is for test and "P" for presentation, "E" for essential, "D" for desirable etc.

Job description - read this next. Where can it help you fill in some more information than you've seen in the person spec? Can you provide examples of when you've already done many of those kinds of tasks or shown similar skills?

Does the Job Description tell you who your main colleagues will be or who might be your key contacts in the role? If so, check out their profiles on LinkedIn – it will help you recognise them at the interview and in the first few days and weeks of your new job.

EXERCISE:

Where do you have an actual or likely "desirable extra / bonus point" to offer?

Can you think of something you've done that might distinguish you from other candidates? What's unique about you?

....

....

....

....

....

....

....

....

....

....

....

How to use the results of your research

All of this "detective work" is to help you to do the very best you can when you are in your interview.

So follow all of the steps and make good notes about the job, the organisation and the sector. As you work through the person specification and the job description think about examples you can give, and then practise what you'll say if they ask you a question related to each skill or competence.

Don't rehearse your answers "off by heart" – you'll sound like a robot if you do that. Instead - make a note of some of your stories so that you at least will remember them when the appropriate moment arrives.

3. What are their Expectations of you?

Based on what you've sent, or said to them in the application process that "won" you this interview, the panel will have some initial expectations.

Interviewing and filling a vacancy is an expensive and time-consuming process for any organisation regardless of its size. Writing job descriptions, advertising the job, shortlisting the applicants, preparing for the interviews, finding the venue, diary space for the interviewer(s), their time – and the time they "lose" interviewing as opposed to doing their "day job", etc, etc.

The interviewer wants the next candidate they see (or hear in a telephone interview) to be a perfect "fit" to the job and the organisation. You need to make it as easy as possible for them to picture you being that "perfect fit".

If your preparation and research – outlined in the previous sections - has been effective and robust you will be better equipped to achieve this. If it's done well you will be ready to fulfil their expectations of you.

As an interviewee, you need to do 3 things for your interviewer(s)

- Reassure

- Flatter

- Avoid distractions

Reassure

You need to help your interviewer to see how brilliant you'll be at doing this job. They need to picture you as the "perfect" candidate for the role. Match what they say they want with exactly what you can offer.

Presenting your most relevant skills and experience, in a way that they can see these as easily transferable, is your aim.

- You need me to do / be / behave like this and this is exactly what I do / can be / have behaved like before.

- They have to be able to see and hear that what they need is exactly what you bring to this role.

32

- This is what you want – this is what I have.

Every answer needs to be a shade of *"yes and"* or *"I have done x which is very like y because..."*

Flatter

This part is about demonstrating your enthusiasm, motivation and how much "homework" you've done on what they need. Show that you really understand the sector / the organisation / the job role in depth. Make sure you know about their recent achievements and accolades.

Show how much you want the job by what you say at the interview. Tell them how keen you are to make a contribution to the great work they're already doing. And sound enthusiastic when you talk to them.

Avoid distractions

Avoid doing or saying things that may be distracting. Ask a friend to give you feedback on whether you fiddle with your hair, scratch your nose or say lots of 'ums' and 'errs'.

Everything you say at interview needs to be as meaningful as possible i.e. every word you use needs to give your interviewer an opportunity to give you another tick or mark in your favour.

Consider which facts about yourself are the most relevant and which are best left unsaid.

Do your homework and try to work out what are they waiting for you to say or demonstrate in your answers. There may be key words or phrases that they need you to mention whilst also demonstrating that you understand their business needs.

Remember to keep your hands under control. A few explanatory gestures are fine but if you use your hands too much the interviewers will stop listening to you. It might help if you keep your hands in your lap, or hold a pen.

And make sure your mobile phone is on silent or – better still - switched off completely!

What's Unique about me?

You need to show you're the solution to their problem and you're exactly what they're looking for. You have to prove that no other candidate brings the same "perfect match" and unique variety / combination of skills and experience.

Think of your interview as an opportunity to demonstrate how "special" you are. You're marketing yourself, and every 'product' should have a USP – that is a "unique selling point". What are your USPs?

So for each aspect of the job role, think about how your experience, knowledge, expertise and skill can "fit" the job and will sound so much better than anyone else can offer.

Always be truthful and focus on the facts – especially where you can quantify the impact you had in a previous role.

Use examples from your current or previous jobs / work experiences, and highlight which particular skills are demonstrated by them - setting out the benefits you will therefore bring to your potential employer.

Help your interviewer to remember you by mentioning something that is truly unique about you. For example, we had a client who had represented her country at the Olympic Games, one who had organised a charity bike ride to China raising millions of pounds in her spare time and another who could speak 3 languages. Each of these was their particular "USP".

EXERCISE:

Take a look at the latest job that you have, and then make a list of all of the reasons why you want to apply for it, and what's special about you.

Incorporate your added "extras" from the previous exercise about desirable versus essential parts of the job description.

The Three Reasons why I am the right person for this job / the strengths I bring are:

1.

2.

3.

The Three Unique things about me / "bonus" things I can offer are:

1.

2.

3.

Make sure these are relevant to the job.

4. How to anticipate / Guess their questions

The job advert, the job description and person specification and now in the digital age – their website should be your starting points for working out what they're likely to ask you.

The key words and phrases should be those they've used to attract you to apply in the first place.

Now it's time for some more "detective work".

Find the key words

You might want to use a highlighter pen (or the equivalent editing software function) to hunt for words and phrases that could be turned into questions.

Predict the Questions

There are different types of questions that can be asked at an interview, such as Competency Based, Strengths Based, technical, or Scenario based. (Some examples of these are set out in the Resources section.) Interviewers may also want to ask a supplementary question based on your answer, such as "what was the challenge for you in that situation?" or "what did you learn from that?".

Many interview questions are structured fairly similarly – e.g.

"Give me an example of when you had experience of x…"

"Tell me about a time when you had to…"

"When have you had to demonstrate x… skill"

There may be a question like:

"What does the word x or phrase x y z mean to you and when have you put this into action?"

This last one is particularly important when the interviewer is trying to work out whether you're going to "fit" into their organisation, how they like to work and their values, culture and behaviours.

See also "Buzzword Bingo" in Chapter 2, and the websites listed in the Resources section.

Be ready for the questions: Why do you want this job? Why this organisation? Why this sector? What can you offer this job?

EXERCISE:

Pick a job you're applying for, work through the job details and note down the likely questions.

Think about the answers you can give that demonstrate the required competences. Build a pool of examples so you can avoid using the same one for every question and demonstrate the breadth of your past experience.

Examples need to be based on your skills and experience and related to the job.

Remember to use "I" rather than "we" when using them. The interviewer is interested in what you did. If you worked as part of a team, tell them what actions you took to achieve the task and which part of it was your sole responsibility.

Use the STAR (Situation, Task, Action, Result) format to help you tell the beginning, middle and end of your answer. Interview questions need you to tell the "story" of how you demonstrated a skill or previous experience. Remember to explain what needed doing, what you did and what happened as a result

Be Aware and Beware

You now know what they <u>should</u> ask you.

Most interviewers are skilled and experienced and during questioning will want to bring the best out of you. However there are people who are very "bad" interviewers. They may do lots of interviewing and still have very poor technique or have their ability limited by "poor" questioning, e.g. Some organisations mistakenly use the same questions regardless of the needs of different vacancies.

As a candidate you need to be prepared in the best possible way. The quality of the interviewer and the interview is not in your control.

Remember also that the quality of an organisation's selection processes may well mirror their culture. So poor interviewing may indicate the quality of other aspects of them as your potential future employer... So be aware and beware.

And some other tips:

- Listen to the question and ask for further clarification if necessary

- Keep answers focussed on the question – try not to waffle

- Go back to a previous question if you remember something you want to add

- If they use a question you consider to be inappropriate then start by checking the relevance and context for it. Legally they're not allowed to ask about things like marital status, childcare etc in the UK – a quick internet search will give you some up to date guidance on what they can or cannot ask. When in doubt about a question clarify their reasoning by asking "how does that relate to my ability to do this job please?"

- Be positive and enthusiastic so the interviewer knows you're really interested in the job role

5. REALISM AND RESILIENCE

Searching for a new job can be time-consuming and tiring, so developing some 'healthy' approaches to the process can help reduce any negative impacts on you.

Being Realistic

Organisations want to secure the best talent by appointing the "top" candidate for the job, and that might mean that another candidate may have just had a little more experience than you, or better skills, or just presented themselves in a more advantageous way.

The important thing to remember is that you've done your best, so if you're unsuccessful don't take it personally.

The interview panel may have a preferred candidate and are just going through the process to appear fair to all and to be opening the opportunity "to the market place".

Interviewers are human – even if this is sometimes difficult to believe! "Humans" are not robotically objective and rational. They can bring their own past experiences, learnt behaviour and preconceptions into the interview with them.

They have to make a decision about whether you will be a good "fit" with the culture of their company.

They may have preconceived ideas about you based on your application, what school or college you went to, or where you live.

Despite the Equalities legislation they may be unwilling to give you a chance based on your gender, ethnicity, age etc. (but of course they won't tell you that!). They may well have no idea that they're applying preconceived ideas to how they judge your performance at interview. This is often referred to as "unconscious bias".

Fortunately many employers now run training for recruitment staff to try to minimize this risk.

Sometimes the interview panel is just dysfunctional; they may each have their own preferred candidate and be using the interview process as a way to score points against each other. If that happens, there's nothing you can do. Think of TV talent shows where one judge doesn't like another so they find ways to comment about contestants / mentees which are meant to annoy their colleagues.

On the other hand there's something known as the "Halo effect" that can work in your favour. For example, if you went to the same school as the interviewer they might assume you're as good as they are at maths.

So it's important to attend each interview with a realistic attitude, and not fall apart if you don't land your dream job first time round.

Remember – when it's "right" for you, you'll be in the "right place at the right time" – although before this happens you will probably have to experience the opposite as well.

Becoming more resilient

Don't get despondent if you don't get the job. Try to become "Resilient" and learn some positive ways to respond after a disappointment or set-back. Resilience is not about not being bothered, but more about being able to recover quickly from a set-back.

There are lots of definitions of this:

> "the ability to succeed personally and professionally in the midst of a high pressured, fast moving and continuously changing environment" *GlaxoSmithKline*

> "the attitude and skill set of an individual allowing them to cope with great efficiency and effectiveness in periods of change and stress." *VIE life*

or   You decide!

So, put more simply, being resilient is about "bouncing back" after a disappointment. And there are some tried and tested steps to help with this.

Useful Reminders

a. Avoid becoming discouraged when things go wrong. Understand that things can go wrong for all sorts of reasons, so develop a habit of shrugging your shoulders and starting again.

b. Remember you can be "in the right place at the right time" or the opposite.

c. The capacity to recover quickly from difficulties = toughness. We will all face some difficulties in our lives. We all need to decide whether to let those "defeat us" forever, or learn ways to help us cope and recover quicker.

d. It's not what happens to you – it's how you choose to perceive it and react to it. You don't have to get all "worked up" just because it's a rainy day – recognise that the weather, and many other things, are out of our control.

e. Control the "controllables" and learn to "let go" of those things that are out of your control. Most times you won't know who the other candidates are, what they can offer that's different to you or what the interviewer's pre-conceptions are about your capability or theirs. But you can control how you feel about the interview, and how much preparation you've done.

f. A little "pressure" may be good for us, while too much can weaken our resolve, so make sure you take steps to keep your stress levels down. Breathe calmly and slowly and try to relax.

g. Optimism helps with resilience – seeing "the glass half-full". It encourages people to feel positive about themselves, about other people, and the world in general.

h. "Solution orientation" – try to develop the ability to see and anticipate potential challenges coming a long way off and to prepare accordingly. It's much easier making plans to deal with possible problems when you're feeling calm and have time to sort things out in advance.

i. Individual accountability – work on developing a strong sense of self-worth and self-regard, which will give you a greater belief in your own abilities.

j. Openness and flexibility – the ability to tolerate, and even thrive on, times of uncertainty will really help you.

k. Managing stress and anxiety – the ability to identify and then deal effectively with potential pressure situations will help you to become more resilient.

l. Aim to be excited rather than nervous!

Using any interview – successful or otherwise – as a learning experience is really helpful.

For this reason it's always worth asking for feedback and using self-reflection.

Asking for feedback

Consider this to be a question to ask at the end of every interview. Also – remember to ask it in this way:

Question to the panel / interviewer: *"Regardless of the outcome of this interview today, who should I ask for feedback please, as I want to improve?"*

Using this structure shows that you want to use this as a learning process and by using "who" you're being more directive and specific. By using an "open question" they have to give you an answer that is longer than just "no".

They may say something like "I'm sorry it's our policy not to give feedback". Even if this is the case at least you've asked the question and know whether or not it's possible to find out how you did, what you did well and what could you have done better etc.

It can be time-consuming to formulate candidate feedback – especially the meaningful kind. And some workplaces just don't have the resource and / or the ability to do this or just don't consider it a priority.

If you're asking for feedback, remember to use open questions such as "in what ways could I have improved....?." rather than closed questions (with a yes/no answer) such as "can I improve?". However, sometimes a direct closed question is the most powerful, such as "can I expect to know the result by the end of today?".

If you ask for specific feedback, such as "what could I have done to answer your questions in a way that would have worked better for you?" that will give them guidance on exactly what you want to improve.

Using "self-reflection"

This is a very useful tool. How do YOU think you did?

It's best to do this as soon as possible after finishing the interview.

As soon as you leave the room or finish the Skype or telephone call, jot down what your initial instinct tells you about how you did. Think about the questions they asked and how you did with your answers while it's fresh in your memory and all the detail is still clear to you.

Think about how you might do things differently or better if that question or scenario came up again.

A simple method is to ask yourself three questions:

- What went well, and why?

- What didn't go so well, and why?

- What could I do better or differently next time?

Now factor in what the interviewer gave you as feedback. How close was it to your own self-assessment? What have you learnt for your next interview?

EXERCISE

Set yourself some reminders

Next time, I will ......

....

....

....

....

....

....

....

....

....

6. AND FINALLY...

We've taken you through how you can think positively, and behave more confidently about your interview, and we then moved on to how to do your research so that you're really well-prepared.

Then we've considered how you're going to anticipate the questions and plan your answers. We all know that not everything will go to plan, so we also discussed how to deal with any possible disappointment.

Now it's your turn to practise ......

"Mirror work" can help you prepare by showing you what you look like as you're answering questions. Simply stand or sit in front of your mirror and talk through some of your potential answers – not to learn them "off by heart", just to make sure that what you say and how you look are in synch.

It's no good talking about being passionate about something if you're looking really bored while you describe it!

If you're being asked to give a presentation, then take plenty of time to prepare. Try using your mobile phone to record yourself. It may be embarrassing to watch back and yet it's probably the best way to reflect on the impression you're about to make at your next interview. It'll help you to avoid any annoying or distracting habits such as twiddling with your hair or jiggling your knee, or hopping from foot to foot.

Be brave – watch it and think of what constructive criticism you can give yourself to improve your "performance".

We hope you've found our book useful and that you've picked up some good tips and techniques to apply at your next interview.

Now you need to put all of this into practice …so get those applications in!

Good luck with your job search. Practise the advice we've given. And enjoy the interview process now that you've learnt how to prepare for success.

RESOURCES

The reference numbers used here relate to the chapters to which they apply.

1. Understanding 'Imposter Syndrome'

This is where you can spend time worrying that people will "find you out", and realise that you're not as good or clever as they thought you were. And that fear can limit your potential, so that you don't even try for jobs that you probably could do very well. It can impact confidence and stifle your ambition.

There are some quite straightforward steps to counter this, one of which is to "be brave" and act as if you were already 100% brilliant at this job and convince yourself they'd be fools not to employ you. You can also ask other people what they think you're capable of, and you'll probably be pleasantly surprised at their answers.

Read "The Secret Thoughts of Successful Women: Why Capable People Suffer from the Impostor Syndrome and How to Thrive in Spite of It" by Valerie Young (Crown Publishing Group, Division of Random House Inc., Nov 2011)

https://hbr.org/2016/07/everyone-suffers-from-imposter-syndrome-heres-how-to-handle-it

Positive Self Talk

Some academics call this NLP (Neuro Linguistic Programming) the principles of which are:

- People are not their behaviour.

- People already possess all the resources they need to succeed and achieve their desired outcomes - they just need to learn how to unlock them.

- The meaning of your communication is found in the response you get. When you learn how to communicate better, the world will respond to you better than ever before.

- You are in charge of your mind - and therefore your life.

- When things get difficult, remember: there is never failure, only feedback.

NLP is based on a strong belief in the possibility of change.

First impressions

They may help or hinder you: Research in the US suggests that where interviewers are well-trained and carry out structured interviews, you're less likely to be judged during the first few moments. However some interviewers aren't so well-trained, and conduct more haphazard interviews, and then they may rely upon their first impressions.

"The structured employment interview: Narrative and quantitative review of the research literature." By Levashina, J., Hartwell, C.J., Morgeson, F.P. and Campion, M.A. (Personnel Psychology, 67(1), pp.241-293. 2014)

"Power Posing"

Amy Cuddy TED talk

https://www.ted.com/talks/amy_cuddy_your_body_language_shapes_who_you_are

"Presence: Bringing Your Boldest Self to Your Biggest Challenges" by Amy Cuddy (Orion, Jan 2016)

PESTLE analysis table

FACTOR	Any recent changes?	What's the impact?
Political		
Economic		
Social		
Technological		
Legal		
Environmental		

Competency Based / Knowledge Skills Experience / Behavioural Style Interviews - Typical Interview Question Keywords

Teamwork

Problem solving / adaptability / response to change

Organisation / planning / under pressure / tight deadlines / juggling priorities

Leadership / developing and coaching others / supervision / line management

"Target driven"

"Customer focused"

Project work / project management

Performance management / quality standard setting / benchmarking

Influencing and negotiation

Policies & procedures / compliance

Finance / budgets / numeracy

Strengths Based Interviews

This approach was developed to overcome people "over-preparing" for competency style questions. It has been pioneered by companies like Ernst & Young to prevent candidates regurgitating standard answers to standard questions.

It aims to uncover the underlying "strengths" of candidates and reveal more of their spontaneous ("true") approach to work, what they enjoy doing, as well as more of their underlying values and personality.

They tend to be shorter questions requiring shorter answers and will feel very different to a competency-based interview.

They may ask things like:

What's a good day? What's a bad day?

Who are your role models?

When did you last go home from work inspired and why?

It relies on a rigorous pre-interview selection process, which ensures only those who meet the highest standards, at least on paper, get through to the face-to-face stage.

It also requires highly-trained interviewers who can discern what strengths are being demonstrated, to what level and how to rank one set of candidate's answers against another's.

5. Being Realistic – The "Halo Effect"

This was named by psychologist Edward Thorndike in reference to a person being perceived as having a "halo", where the positive feelings about one aspect of a person would influence the feelings about the rest of the person (this is called "confirmation bias" by academics).

Becoming more resilient – How to "bounce back" quicker

"Neuroscientific Implications of Psychological Capital: Are the Brains of Optimistic, Hopeful, Confident, and Resilient Leaders Different?" By Suzanne Peterson, Pierre Balthazard, David Waldman and Robert W Thatcher. (Organisational Dynamics, Vol. 37, No. 4.)

"Enhancing Resilience in the Workplace Through the Practice of Caring Relationships" by Sandra Wilson and Shann Shann. (Organisation Development Journal, Winter 2005.)

"Mindset" by Dr Carol S Dweck (Random House 2006)

And here are a couple of academic definitions:

Researchers Wilson & Ferch (2005) emphasised the importance of mental flexibility and creativity: "Resilience refers to the psychological ability to let go of old internal structures of thinking and behaving that over the years have given us a sense of stability and coherence; as well, resilience refers to our ability to create and reintegrate new structures of thinking and behaving that provide us a more mature sense of coherence".

Peterson and others (2011) saw a link between ways the brain and body respond in leaders: "Resilient individuals are characterised by a staunch view of reality. They are very logical in their interpretations of setbacks—what is in their control, out of their control, and options for taking action. Finally, this brain activity leads to the development of "realistic" optimism as well as the motivational processes involved for pursing the courses of action related to confidence and the strategies devised for overcoming life's obstacles."

Useful websites

www.121interviewcoaching.co.uk
www.anitapickerden.co.uk
www.linkedin.com
www.glassdoor.co.uk
www.mindtools.com

You might also want to take a look at Career Sidekick's 128 Interview Questions to practice: http://careersidekick.com/common-job-interview-questions

ABOUT THE AUTHORS

Claire - Owner of "One to One Interview Coaching"

"I have the best job in the world helping clients prepare for job interviews by coaching them to unlock their confidence, secure an impact and then practise what they'll say. I consider it a privilege to be able to work with people at major turning points in their lives."

With over 25 years' experience of interviewing in the private, public and charity sectors she works with clients all over the world through the 'magic' of Skype or FaceTIme and with all age groups from teenagers and University undergraduates right through to the over 60s.

She's helped people to get jobs in sectors as diverse as: banking, aviation, legal, automotive, civil service, IT / data analysis, health, media, sport, public utilities and into academia.

Claire's clients are now working for organisations as wide ranging as:

Ernst and Young, BBC, NATO, Dyson, Sky, KPMG, Jaguar Land Rover, Thomson Airways, NHS, Sport Wales, Royal Mail, Capita, Electoral Commission, Welsh Water, Time Out, Savills UK, TES Global, Camden

Council, Roche, Crown Prosecution Service, RAF Cosford, Leeds Beckett University, Robin Hood Airport …and the list goes on

Guardian Careers regularly use Claire as an "Expert Panelist" for live web chats on anything job interview related.

She lectures at both the University of Worcester and the University of Wolverhampton.

Claire was a National "Investors in People" Award winner for her staff development and recruitment work at The Countryside Agency and is Civil Service Job Interview Panel trained – the Gold Standard in its sector

claire@121interviewcoaching.co.uk www.121interviewcoaching.co.uk

Anita – Director of Anita Pickerden Associates Ltd., and Work Horizons Ltd.

Dr Anita Pickerden was a lecturer in Further Education Colleges and Universities, designing and delivering high quality training programmes in Leadership and Management. She continues to teach in these areas, mainly in a work-based environment, for example on Executive Education programmes and managing Work Based Project modules on a Retail Management degree.

Her PhD research shows that good work life balance can improve employee engagement and she works with associates to improve productivity and work performance through training; coaching and evaluation. Her company offers Work Life Balance and Resilience coaching programmes.

Anita trained with the Centre for Coaching from 2004-2007, gaining qualifications in Coaching, Psychological Coaching, Coaching for Performance, Organisational Stress Management and Coaching for Health & Wellbeing. She also holds a Diploma and Advanced Diploma in NLP & Health from Central NLP.

She has coached people in preparing for interviews since 2015, and helps individuals to get themselves 'work-ready' through an online support network called Work Horizons.

anita@pickerden.co.uk   http://anitapickerden.co.uk

Anna – Director of New Possibilities Ltd, specialising in graphic facilitation and graphic recording techniques, creating visual minutes of events, team days, engagement events, conferences and strategic planning meetings.

She has developed considerable skills in facilitation, mediation and conflict management. By listening closely to what is important; and helping individuals and groups to identify the change they would like to see; Anna helps to represent people's views in a constructive and supportive way. By clarifying thinking, making visual connections and reflecting the key messages in discussions groups have been successful in reaching principled solutions.

anna@newpossibilities.co.uk   www.newpossibilities.co.uk